EAT OR WE BOTH STARVE

Victoria Kennefick grew up in Cork and lives in Kerry. Her pamphlet *White Whale* won the Munster Literature Centre Chapbook Competition in 2014 and the Saboteur Award for Best Poetry Pamphlet in 2015. She was named an Arts Council Next Generation Artist in 2016. Her poems have appeared in *Poetry Magazine*, *PN Review*, *The Poetry Review*, *Poetry Ireland Review*, *The Stinging Fly* and elsewhere.

Eat
Or
We
Both
Starve

VICTORIA KENNEFICK

CARCANET

First published in Great Britain in 2021 by
Carcanet
Alliance House, 30 Cross Street
Manchester, M2 7AQ
www.carcanet.co.uk

A CIP catalogue record for this book is
available from the British Library.

ISBN 978 1 80017 070 4

Book design by Andrew Latimer
Printed in Great Britain by SRP Ltd, Exeter, Devon

The publisher acknowledges financial
assistance from Arts Council England.

CONTENTS

To my beloved mother Úna.
Thank you for everything.
This is for you.

EAT OR WE BOTH STARVE

'Alas, what wickedness to swallow flesh into our own flesh, to fatten our greedy bodies by cramming in other bodies, to have one living creature fed by the death of another! In the midst of such wealth as earth, the best of mothers, provides, nothing forsooth satisfies you, but to behave like the Cyclopes, inflicting sorry wounds with cruel teeth! You cannot appease the hungry cravings of your wicked, gluttonous stomachs except by destroying some other life.'

– Ovid, *Metamorphoses*, trans. by Mary M. Innes (1955)

LEARNING TO EAT MY MOTHER, WHERE MY MOTHER IS THE TEACHER

Where did I start?

Yes, with the heart, enlarged,
its chambers stretched through caring.
In this body feeling
is what the body *is*.
The alert heart, an alarm rings
out in all hours of the night,
flashing red and white.
Oh is it in defiance or defeat, I don't know,
I eat it anyway, raw, still warm.
The size of my fist, I love it.

Strange, a vegetarian resorting to cannibalism.

She is disgusted with me.

Wouldn't you begin with the outside?

Sweating, I pry open the rib cage.

I do not want to eat her ribs, but I do.
Then strip her fingers of meat.
I hold them tenderly
in my mouth, watch her blue eyes
well-up out of love, I assume.
I move from heart, to ribs, fingers,
to spongy lungs: buoyant,
porous, melt-in-the-mouth.

The eyes are tougher than expected,
aqueous humour slithers down my throat.
A surprise, it's minty.

I know what you're thinking, I left the brain.

No, not so. I have consumed
that organ piecemeal, sweet
morsels since my teeth came in, it tastes
like the sound
of sirens you don't know
are screaming until they suddenly stop.

(M)EAT

I sucked marrow from bones at dinner,
my father's face a bloody grin of pride. I ate liver in chunks
for breakfast, pink and firm, jewels to adorn my insides.
I gloried in the feel of flesh, the exertion of the chew.
Holding my mother's hand in the English Market,
I saw them – turkey chandeliers, plucked,
bruised purple eyelids dainty lightbulbs.
Their smell, fresh as the insides of my mouth.
Mother stroked my hair. *There, there.* I refused to eat
meat, became pillowy, meek. She hid muscle under mashed potato,
I tasted its tang in soup. *Eat up*, my parents said. I could not
swallow. My skin goose-pimple yellow, doctors drew blood
in tiny, regular sips. Teeth turned to glass and shattered
in my mouth. All I could taste was blood.

A YOUNG GIRL DISCOVERS HER REFLECTION

I saw her face all the time, mistook it for mine; little mirror said nothing.
That should have been the first sign. I got stuck at what parts of each other
we would share. *I want your hair*, I'd say. She would smile, dress her doll.

I was eight when we wore the same outfit to church, but couldn't match
her pony-tail sway up the aisle. After Mass, adults cast their gaze down,
eye-scales weighing us. I watched how distorted and untidy I became

in glass diamonds on the chapel door; the priest called me *a big girl*.
I want to be you in every reflective surface, boxed in. Instead I stare at a plump
face I do not recognise, its green eyes replicate. I try on your tiny pointed smile

CORPUS CHRISTI PROCESSION

That May
I collected
rose-heads
to peel off
their petals,
and lay them deep
in my new wicker basket
lined with linen.
Dressed in white,
God's little bride,
I plucked out
each petal
and kissed it,
the Communion
wafer still stuck
to my palate.
Winding up
and down
the faithful hills
of Ballycotton
I festooned the path
for priests to trample
all the petals brown.
I had been so careful
not to bruise them
with my lips.
Other girls sniggered
behind cupped hands,

whispered through
lacy fingers,
as my petals
rushed
to the ground
to die,
*She's really
kissing them.*

SWING

Push me higher until I am all stomach,
until my eyes are like that fist of muscle,
tight and hungry. Fill me with green fields for sky.

Push me higher until I am all fingertips
feeling to the top, to the roof of our house calling, *Mother, watch!*
And she will, from the kitchen window, rinsing lettuce in the sink.

Push me higher until I am giddy from kicking clouds and birds,
burning my shoes off the sun, just push me.
The ropes vibrate, I barely hold them – let them sing.

When I touch the ground again, my legs feel like running.

SWIMMING LESSON

the day I almost drowned
mother pulled me out
of the ocean by my hair

the world blurry with seawater
air wet and my lips blue without
I was not sure

I was alive – my eight-year-old
chest tight and sore
it surprised me

how quick
the surrender
underwater

I could see myself
a baby in a bubble
ultrasound

the bubble simmered
a tiny heart pulsed
in and out like a wave

it didn't count
that sun once baked my skin
to contentment

that I liked cats or yellow jumpers
stitches prepared
to unravel

start again – I resurfaced on sand
little sister knelt beside me
father called my name

wanting to die
salty droplets
trembled on my skin

HUNGER STRIKES CATHERINE OF SIENA (1347–1380)

My sister taught me how.
Oh Bonaventura, they wanted
me to marry him, the slack-jawed widower.

I vomited twigs, hid in the convent,
wore a widow's habit. The other nuns complained
until at twenty-one I met Him.

He presented me with a ring fashioned from His skin.
Told me this sliver of flesh bound us;
wait, He told me, promising it would be special.

I levitated; only ate His body, others did not
understand how good it was
to kiss His holy prepuce.

Oh, Bonaventura, I am a house of sticks,
my bones rattle with desire until I lick it.
I feel it quiver, alive on my tongue.

CHOKE

I want to hold things in my mouth –
a key,
               buttons,
a fingernail,
               the click of a boiled sweet
against enamel.
               A toddler I stole my mother's pills,
               prised the lid off the bottle with tiny teeth,
               arranged the capsules by colour and size.
               My mother panicked when she found me,
               tablets skittled on the bedspread.
                       At the hospital the nun
                       held the cup of charcoal to my mouth,
                       I spat black into a white bowl.
                       Its burnt taste,
                       I thought I must be bad.

A child, given a boiled sweet by a cousin,
I popped it in
       my mouth,
turned
               a dainty shade
of blue.
               My father spun me upside-down,
               the sweet shaken loose.
               In another version, my mother
               pushes the sweet down
               my throat with a finger, or maybe

that was when I was three
and nearly choked
in a different cousins' house
gagging on another boiled sweet.
Maybe

that's what I'm looking for –
my mother's finger
            down my throat,
pushing
            sugar
deep into me.

SECOND COMMUNION

The altar boy tinkles the bell.
Father Madden enters, his chasuble fluid as milk;
a shaft of sunlight pierces the Christ embroidered in tinsel –

(that feeling
not hunger)

My mother, in her mink coat, smells of the expensive perfume my father buys
in duty-frees. He is next to her in tweed, then my little sister – a frill.
Father Madden reads a gospel, in my tummy a throb –

(unwrap it
not thirst)

Burying my face deep into the pelt of my mother's coat, musk
tussles with the sweet incense of prayer. My head rises as the priest lifts the host –
I see the cut of it, that tiny moon –

(I don't want to eat
any body)

If I eat Jesus will he want to eat me?
Think on that, not the chalice sloshing with blood. Soon it will be time
to stutter up the aisle, open my mouth and be fed –

FORTY DAYS

Sister, let's unwrap Lent like a treat,
stroke the smooth chocolate egg beneath,
the one that we couldn't eat;
the wafer, yes, but no ice-cream.
Little Jesuses in the desert with no dessert.
The devil tapping on our flat-black
windowpane before bed; mother, cutting
tiny slices of bread in the kitchen corner,
eating from doll plates. She couldn't be prouder
of our ecstasy of denial, little letter-box lips
refusing the sins of the tongue.
Easter bells rattled the glass, Christ has risen, Alleluia.
Resurrection with chocolate sauce made us sick,
giddy pupils rising in our irises, yours
the most divine Holy-Mary blue. We held hands,
spun around, fizzy-headed, falling down.
Open the chocolate box, sister, see liquor-centred
grown-up sweets. Pillows of sin, full
with seven deadly tastes, a menu read to us on waking.

In the Ordinary Time of your dark kitchen,
we drop tissuey tea bags into boiled water.
Rust whispers to transparency. Peace blooms,
bleeding into molecules, slowly.

DOLL GAME

I enjoyed nodding
my Barbies' heads vigorously
so the toggle allowing them to bow
broke each moulded neck.
The sound of the crack reassuring.
I collected the shards
in a small velvet purse,
pushed the heads down hard
on the splintered stumps
to re-capitate. Each Barbie
neckless but alive.
Then I chopped off
their hair with a safety scissors
and presented such a doll
to my sister on her birthday.

She stripped her naked
as a new-born, brought her
to the beach to baptise her.
It wasn't cold.

My birthday too,
I carried my box-fresh Barbie
tight in my small white fist,
encouraged her to look up
and down, back and forth
along the sand. Testing her,

the tan plastic that made her,
I tugged at her blonde strands
already loose. Though I pointed
out my sister to her on the shoreline,
her long hair whipping
around her head, a tiny storm –
though I gestured out to sea,
to the neckless doll's head bobbing
in grey November waves, she didn't blink.

BEACHED WHALE

At first I thought that enormous lump of red-brown on the sand
was the trunk of some ancient, washed-up tree.

It was only when I mounted the object,
digging my small hands into something far too pliable,
that it really hit me, the stale smell of a thousand low tides

and the mute open mouths of the many onlookers
with their hysterical dogs, the seagulls circling like squalling clouds,
my mother's curlew scream as she ran towards me, disjointed.

Astride the whale like this,
looking at my mother move through dimensions,
planes of distance,

I thought of boutique dressing rooms brimming
with clothes and tension, like gas, expanding. And of two little girls
watching their mother cry at her reflection distorted in a fluorescent mirror.

The weight of her past made flesh on her hips,
the scars of our arrivals barely healed after all this time,
my blind hands all over the body.

Grasping, desperate to hold onto something real,
not knowing what that was.

LIGHTHOUSE

They say that when they laid his bloated body
in her arms she tried to dry him
with her long red hair; her tears
threatened to drown him all over again.

They say that when she finally let go
her fingers were puckered;
in the morning her hair was pure white.
She never left the corner house again.

They say her bones barely held up pale skin,
sail-taut against the storm of winds
that prevailed night after night,
she fell away to nothing.

They say she haunted windows,
watched the water, her face a perfect sphere.
And the crews sailing the rising sea
often mistook her for the moon.

HUNGER STRIKES ANGELA OF FOLIGNO (1248–1309)

I drink pus from wounds of the unclean.
Christ, it is like water to me, sweet
as the Eucharist.
> I pick
> at their scabs, chew them flat
> between my teeth.
The lice I pluck and let drown
on my tongue sustain me.
Lord, I am the Host.
> Lead me in the light
> to the summit of perfection.
> I will pray and pray
and pray to you: to remain poor,
be obedient, chaste and humble.
This is all I ask. God-man, feed me.

SECOND FAMILY

i.   *Widowers don't stay that way for long*

It is like this

wedding dresses over

brides' heads, born-again

hands reaching through

silk and lace, another woman's

children ready-made waiting.

Two brides, four brides

lit like lanterns float up the aisle

toward grooms. The same men.

My grandfather, my father

hold the same hands.

Again. First wives, delicate,

wilt like flowers in late summer,

storybook wives their long hair

disappears, curling in

and out of photographs.

My family matrimony squared.

My grandmother a second. My mothe

too. Rearranging pieces,

the pattern ill-fitting. So much

white. Their veils slip again.

Again. Again.

ii.   *The wicked stepmother is my (m)other is me*

What if I were to tell you my mother
stepped into that space
left by another, like her mother
before her, like a question mark, curved
like that. Am I wicked too,
nasty half-sister with grabby hands?
I cracked the glass slipper,
I didn't mean to (though I am
always stealing; I squander
my life like coins.) Our maternal line
starving (we still eat apples,
we are immune).

I never heard my father
say her name. I wrote it down instead,
swallowed the paper like a host. Even now,
I flinch if I hear it on the radio, read it in a book,
meet someone with it on them
like a wine stain. I love her because
I am here. My hands should be cut off.
I am here. I should be blinded, locked
in a tower, sent into the desert.
I am here. I should be left
to choke on fruit. Be put to sleep,
my veins split with a glass shard.
A thief, a thief I stole
her space. Not my mother. It was *her*

I replaced.

iii.   *I am cuckoo*

cupped my ears every spring to hear
    that ridiculous call

        weird bird
           whose name I twisted round my finger

loopy thing
    wandering voice I tried to catch

        once a dim shape
           suspended over fields.

You were on an open perch, a rock
    by a stream – a tease with raised tail

        your iris dead yellow. I
           didn't know then you disguise

yourself, invade small birds' nests
    shunt out an egg. That, once born, your chick

        prods others out, makes a begging call
           like a whole brood. I stood still

as a reed, curled out a cuckoo-voice, loud
    sonic eruption from a space

        between my diaphragm and sinuses. Together
        we replicated an infinite hoop

familiar sound, whistle
of my half-siblings' hearts plummeting

to earth, small wreckages smashed on lino
to be crushed again by my smug baby finger.

I did nothing but grow
bigger and bigger

my mouth open.

iv.   *Extension*

Bungalow on a hill squints out to sea
          through an embarrassment of windows,
the drapes semi-drawn so they can't catch us
          as we balance on those sills, stretching
to see waves crash on Ardnahinch beach.
          We press our lips against the glass;
our smudgy patterns bleed as we breathe
          and breathe.

                              *

With footsteps light as a cat's, my little sister padded through
the extension's freshly poured concrete in new summer sandals,
the ones with daisies punched through – her toes, petals on the lip.

The sun gawped at her perfect shiny hair. Louise, I watched you
stand in the middle of that grey square, a fluttering tissue
in white, your fringe kissing the long, curious curl of your eyelashes.

                              *

At night, the lighthouse beam steals in to stroke
          our faces, on blind days the foghorn's moan
reminds us it is not our house. Sister and me:
          an infestation. We eat everything like moths
in a woollen carpet, munching through memories that are not ours.
          We hide photo albums, stuff the tiny wedding dress
to the back of the hot press. Bury strange adolescent treasures
          in the garden – a badge, a pipe, a cassette tape.

*

your creamy contentment at reaching the centre, and remaining
there, a spell, until our mother saw you, roared at the builder,
then at me – never at you, how could she? And waded in past

the wooden boundary, going to you as you set in concrete, bending
down to unstrap the beautiful sandals, small monuments to your bravery
encrusted on the foundation, where the mantelpiece would be.

*

Detached, we imitate clouds in the extension, manifest
        as tiny intruders in pyjamas running down the hall.
We slip into beds our father's first family slept in,
        we don't know any better, rooms flash red through curtain-splits.
We don't know any better, we were born afterwards. Because of.
        In our dreams we tumble towards the sea. Because of.
Our salty little lips disrupting glass with wings of breath
        can't seem to shape the word *sorry*.

*

Landed back on tarmac you grinned neat milk teeth at me,
sobbed a little to our mother, waved to your sandals as if from a train.

v.   *Hochelaga: or it doesn't matter now, we have all gone*

I discovered in the end
the hill our house is built on
is not natural, my father created
it filling-in the gully with stubborn rocks.
Such things one does to make a home.

ALTERNATIVE MEDICINE

I am here to heal, to confess to that darkness
standing in front of my eyes when I open them,

that food squirms as if alive with maggots,
that I have shut my mouth to everything but words.

The therapist taps my shoulders, my head, my knees,
tells me I was a nun once, very strict.

This makes sense; I know how cleanly I like
to punish myself. Also, a Celtic priestess;

I hope I had red hair, that I ate men
like air, all that jazz.

She moves to my forehead; her fingers drum
on my skin. There were two of you, she says.

My body remembers in a jolt, the guilt
black and endless. It is a tunnel.

No, it is someone else's shadow. Almost like mine.
A twin, poor thing. In my mother's womb

I consumed this sibling, she says, like I gnaw
at my flesh now, my body feeding on whatever scrap.

You didn't do it, she says. *I know I did,*
I know I did. My little twin, one of us had to go.

CURE FOR ANAEMIA

Don't touch me – I will snap
and crumble,

I am missing something. My head
a barking dog; rabid, it drools.

My lousy wrists limp
against the table's edge, I shiver

at a plate. The cloth it rests on,
starched stiff like a shroud,

the bone china heavy with flesh.
I say again, I am deficient.

My pallor wrong, the tablets not enough
to make me red.

The doctors recommend I eat it,
the muscle and fat I've avoided since I was eight.

Will my body remember the tough
and tender give of corporeal mass?

I take a bite. It is my own stomach
in boneless pieces. I screw up

my eyes, furry inside, filled
with butcher's flies. I cry, my throat

refuses peristalsis. The fist of meat remains,
I smell it when breath escapes.

I push the plate away; see its match
in the docile moon, porcelain.

COUNT UGOLINO OR HISTORY'S VAGUEST CANNIBAL

Ugolino, locked up
with your children in that tower,

dreaming you were all wolves
hunted and torn to pieces, gnawing

at your fingers in grief or hunger.
The only sound that of doors

being nailed shut. What did you do
when they begged you to eat them?

When they cried out, *Stop our suffering.*
You brought us into being dressed in this sad flesh,

now strip it all away. Their scrawny limbs reaching
towards you, heads limp with exhaustion,

a lack of light. Four dead children,
you so blind by the sixth day you spoke

to them as though they were alive. Hunger,
you say, proved stronger than grief.

SELFIE

Sitting alone in the house eating
my fingernails/watching the sky
move away. The room is full/versions of me
crouching on the floor/balancing on the windowsill/
reclining on the pout of my lower lip/
asleep in the crease of my eyelid.
Not alone/with myself/A snare /I have been
running from   I do not live
the way humans are supposed to,
compare my face to others you know.
I fall short/an embarrassing fringe/No matter
what face I try on   it's exhausting.
All versions shake our heads.
There is much to do/until we think we are not
What We Are: Victoria(s). I see
those letters written on envelopes I know
are for me   because of the shape
of that word/that greedy V –
its two arms open wide/ready
to accept anything.

HUNGER STRIKES VERONICA GIULIANI (1660–1727)

My confessor ordered her to do it,
the novice kicked me again and again.

Her shoe pummelled my teeth,
bloodied my lips. I did not stir
or whimper, I kept my mouth open.

I remained bruised for weeks.

When my face was almost pink again
He prompted me to clean the walls and floor

of my cell with my tongue. I licked
for hours, scraping up each wisp of skin and hair.
My throat became thick with cobwebs,

my mind clear as light.

RESEARCHING THE IRISH FAMINE

*

Bulldozers disturb the old workhouse site,
uncover babies' skulls
curved like tiny moons. Their mothers
beside them, lullabies
locked in their jaws.

*

They can measure hunger now. Test
how much bellies rumbled, the stress
teeth were under, rotten
before they broke
scurvied gums.

*

Mothers exhausted their own bodies
to produce milk. High nitrogen
evidence of body tissue
breaking down,
recycling.

*

The starving
human
literally
consumes
itself.

*

Babies died
anyway. They all died. Wasted away
like potatoes
in the ground. The whole
country rotten.

*

What was left buried in memorial gardens,
alongside statues to honour hunger:
children with milky fat,
teeth in braces.
All we do now is eat.

CORK SCHOOLGIRL CONSIDERS THE GPO, DUBLIN 2016

I am standing outside the GPO
in my school uniform, which isn't ideal.

My uniform is the colour of bull's blood.

In this year, I am sixteen, a pleasing symmetry
because I love history, have I told you that?

It is mine so I carry it in my rucksack.

I love all the men of history sacrificing
themselves for Ireland, for me, these rebel Jesuses.

I put my finger in the building's bullet holes;

poke around in its wounds.
I wonder if they feel it,

those boys,

I hope they do, their blooming faces
pressed flat in the pages of my books.

I lick the wall as if it were a stamp,

it tastes of bones, this smelly city,
of those boys in uniforms,

theirs bloody too. I put my lips

to the pillar. I want to kiss them all. And
I do, I kiss all those boys goodbye.

THE TALK

when I asked what that word meant
I was directed to the dictionary.
My older half-sister showed me
the entry; her grave thumb covered
all the interesting bits

when my best friend climbed a tree
in our front garden her knickers flashed,
the gusset soiled rust-red; I said nothing
but she didn't come out to play
for five whole days

when our science teacher told us to open
the pinkest chapter, all I could think of was
Michelangelo's *David* but Mr. Kelly keeled over
on the wooden stool, his forehead
kissing bare plastic tile

but when a man, older than me
in double-denim, sucked the alcopop
tongue out of my head,
shoved his hands under the clefts
of my bottom

I figured it out.

BIG GIRL

In the nightclub   I drank
Peach Schnapps   with ice
my heart   a nest of eggs
I wanted   all of you
to see   my tender belly
and not be   ashamed
I showed   only peacock eyes
my big   fuchsia   mouth
I wanted   to fill up
with the floppy compliance   of beautiful   wet tongues
flashing   in and out
under lights   Outside
after   kissing some   of you
or trying to   ample
for all   of you
I sucked chips   salty and bitter
gathered those   who remained
starving   too drunk to walk
home   into a circle
Around   I went   parting
lips   pushing masticated potato
onto the dent   of your   plump tongues
My saliva   in your stomachs
(stirring)
My pulse in   your necks
(hatching)

SUPPER

You slosh oil and wine, your loose tongue purple,
you spill about the ex you courted in Kilmainham Gaol Museum –
the two of you stuffing envelopes with invitations
to an opening. Your mouth went dry from licking.

In exchange this ex let you touch Maud Gonne's dress.
You take another sip; I want to eat all the lubricated lettuce
in the bowl, it sheens in candlelight,
my clothes are getting tight. *Was she tiny?* I ask; *She was*, you whisper.

I wonder if, for all your licking, you got to finger
more intimate garments, still warm. I shift in my chair,
radicchio winks; nothing on the table but
greens, a drained glass, your words decanting.

n the Dark Fetish Network,
og in under an assumed name.
elish online chats
ith a fourteen-year-old,
u will find Lindsay-Su
n my hard-drive,
ked on a plate, apple in her mouth.
ven at primary school I thought about
king girls
  the kitchen.

My mother was very domineering,
made a drunken pass at me.
when I was fifteen.
I don't dislike other women as a result.
I have never discussed this predilection
with my wife. She doesn't care
for cooking,
I enjoy preparing food. I wonder
what it would be like to eat a girl
She has.

THE PREACHER'S DAUGHTER

We drink too much pineapple rum, straight from the bottle,
bitch about the red-haired girl, the fetish model,
a preacher's daughter with a thing for unreasonable shoes.

From her faded patchwork quilt, bleeding
hearts, we watched her mutate into a PVC Alice Liddell.
How did she manage in seven-inch patent heels?

She was tall as wheat – or the ceiling was low.
Cradling a mewing ginger-ball, she kissed the mirror
where their confederate-blue eyes

matched. Three scars began to scab on her arm,
deep big-cat scrawls she told us she cut herself
because it's art and her clients like her

that way. We followed her clip-clop down
the rabbit hole; me, to hear tales of her running track
in those shoes; you, to see her white skin even paler

under lights. Back in your dorm room, I am static.
You pay to watch her pixelated Snow White online;
complain her constant chatter ruined it, or her, for you.

IN MEMORY OF MARY TYLER MOORE

As Laura Petrie, stay-at-home TV mom,
wife to Dick Van Dyke, Mary Tyler Moore
refused to wear dressy skirts,
frou-frou heels, or pearls. Laura wore pants,
specifically capris because, *Women don't wear
full-skirted dresses to vacuum in.*

Studio heads wrung their hands. She looked good.
She looked so good they were afraid. Afraid
housewives would be angry that Laura and/or
Mary looked too good in pants. Sponsors were concerned
about the fit of her pants, using the term, *cupping under*
which Mary Tyler Moore assumed meant,
My, you know, my seat –

That there was a little too much definition.
They tried to limit the *cupping under*
as much as possible. Mary Tyler Moore, aka Laura,
was not allowed to wear pants in more than one scene.
Three episodes it lasted until they grew lazy
and forgetful. There were no riots,

there was definitely *cupping under*.
Suits nodded their balding heads.
She got absolution from men everywhere.
Women breathed a sigh of relief too:
that's what they wore at home. We all vacuum
in pants now, and then.
                              And then, and now
our pert bottoms sway in unison, pants
cupping under and everyone watching.

HUNGER STRIKES COLUMBA OF RIETI (1467–1501)

My body is a temple I keep
clean for You, spotless –
lashing my skin so it grows

tired of bleeding.
Wearing hair shirts I cannot forget
what it means to be alert.

I have toured the Holy Land in visions.
I don't imagine they would understand
what I see.

When they came for me, the men,
they ripped off my robes
expecting to find me virginal,

untouched.
How they gasped in horror!
How glad I was that I had used myself

like an old rag.
Beating myself with that spiked
chain shielded me,

my breasts and hips so deformed
they ran from me,
screaming.

DIET

In the hospital, my father ate tubs of high-calorie
strawberry-flavoured meal-replacement.
Occasionally, vanilla. Sometimes, they brought
meals under plastic covers with stewed tea.
The whole ward a nightmare of hard-boiled eggs
and jelly. He would have starved
were we not on-call to lift up his head in our hands,
talk nonsense, distract him from the truth
of how he was living. With his eyes shut, he opened
his mouth a little, so we fed him with tiny spoons.
How could he eat it, this gloopy mass, sliming
the carton? In truth, I fell out of love with food
because my father did. It was summer, I remember.
I wanted to pick life from trees, wellness from bushes,
huge bunches of health from the garden and hold them
to his lips so he could taste sun, air, light, his life
still throbbing in my veins. But everything died
when I brought it inside that room. Still
I marvel how death turned me too to bone.

ARCTIC CIRCLE

My father's brain filleted
on the icy X-ray block

glows luminescent, a strange fish on a slab.
I shiver at this part of him

I never thought I'd see.
His neural pathways presented in a grin

we shared on Sundays by the sea,
watching birds scatter air when he clapped his hands.

The surgeon explains how meningiomas
develop. *They don't so much grow within it*

but rather push the brain away. He points with a thick finger,
Here. And here. Where the circle is broken.

The surgeon says, *It is the size of a bird egg.* I am too scared
to ask which type. My father would prefer

a seagull or curlew. *Atypical,*
the surgeon says, *faster growing, likely to grow back.*

My father's brilliant network of networks.
Now, just the sound of ice splitting.

JANUARY

I have begun the purge.
Month of hunger,
raindrops fall
from window sills, ice
slithers in puddles,
the smoky breath of animals
greets the air. Morning's back
already broken, veins
obvious on everything.
Emptying myself
of all things ripe
and wanton, I am winter grass.
Observe me survive
as earth's shoulder blades
that jut, cut up the sky
that pushes down on all of us
as if it wants to die.
See, I am transparent
as sunrise.
Starving, I count
my bones as valuable.

RIB

I have visited your grave many times expecting to find you
tending your plot, maybe with a shovel or a strimmer,
turning your handsomely-lined face towards the sun.

In Kilmahon cemetery, wild garlic excretes a heavy smell.
White bonnets bob at your wooden cross,
embarrassed to show their faces, roots grown so deep.

Reflected in the bronze plaque, my borrowed face,
my something blue. Your name, that date
engraved above pebbles surfaced, shyly, in the wake.

I see through soil and rotting wood to what remains of you,
with bare hands I'll dig, scavenge your grave goods.
Count, collect, wash your bones, knit them together,

taste dirt under my fingernails, earth that reeks of ramsons.
The whole empty, swallowed, to fill with rainwater
and white feathers. Wild garlic lingers,

a confusion of scents and sense. You pull your weeds,
in your element. Heaviness tugs at me, you do too.
A corset I wear made of your ribs, my rib that made you.

I DIDN'T KNOW WHAT TO DO WITH MYSELF

I told a twelve-year-old he was annoying
he found our class trip to a medieval castle
boring
I asked him what he thought medieval castles were supposed to do
as if everything should entertain
he shrugged
I put an asterisk
beside his name in my roll book to pretend
I cared

I was shrill with a colleague who, I'm sure, doesn't like me
I drove home too fast
there was nothing for dinner
I ate raw celery from the bag didn't wash it
there were squashed flies on it like eyelashes

I didn't brush my teeth fuzzed with bacteria
There was no time
Instead I bit my nails to the quick imagined them
stabbing me
my own
tiny person trying to get out
I bumped my head off the wall
to feel something
saw stars.

A YOUNG GIRL CONSIDERS HER GRANDMOTHER, BALLINAMONA 1921

Two slipped stitches at the end of a row,
nothing after my sister and me,
two birds falling out of a tree.

My grandmother sits at the window
by the sea, knitted to her mourning shawl,
her hair a wispy halo of smoke.

When she stands free, it's at ninety degrees
her bones brittle as burnt paper.
I thought she was searching

for something at her feet, admiring
her reflection in her lace-up patent leather shoes.
My sister's face shining in them too

a thousand years from now, those eyes,
interrogation-blue. She is so old
it makes me want to dig up graves.

Peg, there you are putting it all in place
pinning washing to the line in Ballinamona.
Eighteen, and smiling wide with a mouth full of sky,

secrets stuffed up your sleeve
like cotton hankies, a brace of boys
crammed up the chimney,

flying columns grounded in soot.
Your own brother in a cage
but the clothes are clean and your breath wordless

and reliable as your knees are on the tuffet at mass
every Sunday. Those sheathed boys
know your metronome heart. Know you, and all the Pegs.

Margaret, Maggie, Peg, Granny.
I am not a child, but trying to be
or I'll rip off my skin with grief.

Pages lost, photographs untaken,
gunshots, stand-offs locked up
in delicate lips so fine and thin

they let nothing out, or nothing in.
For now, I'll climb onto your lap
against bird bones.

Under your black shawl I'll make a nest.
With each heart pulse time's loose threads
unravel at my cheek.

Tell me everything,
I will be safe like they were.
I imagine you standing tall and straight, aflame.

PYTHAGOREANS

You know how this begins –
the square of the hypotenuse is equal
to the sum of the square on the opposite two sides.

The human digestive system resembles that of other
plant eaters. Never any good at sums
even you know that your stomach is an equation,

that Pythagoras was a vegetarian who lived on
bread and honey, so was stable and sweet.
Another Pythagorean equation – you are what you eat.

Pythagoras also argued that the steak on your plate could be
the searing flesh of your great-grandmother, that spirits migrate
from humans to animals like dust to carpet.

Yet another equation, this time for the transmigration of souls.
Pythagoras argued that such cruelty sticks. Ghosts hover
about your shoulders, whisper poison in your ears.

Being brutal does something to a person. But if you wanted to stay out
of trouble in Ancient Greece then better to hide yourself behind a slab
of meat. That's what Seneca did. That's what Ovid did.

You know how this ends – not so, Pythagoras
starving in a field of beans was slaughtered by his enemies.
He considered them all relatives, blood splattered on every pulse.

HUNGER STRIKES GEMMA GALGANI (1878–1903)

Chapter 12: Attacks by the Devil[1]

Chapter 13: St. Gemma's Gift is Raised on the Wings of
Contemplation to the Highest Degree of Divine
Love[2]

Chapter 14: St. Gemma's Last Sickness[3]

Chapter 15: St. Gemma's Death and Burial[4]

---

1 All night I dream of food, Jesus take my taste from me. Rip out
my tongue and I will expiate, through my bleeding for you, all the sins
committed by your shrouded men.
2 For sixty days I vomited whenever I ate.
3 I was tormented by banquets.
4 Am I threatened by flesh or its opposite?

PARIS SYNDROME

The Eiffel Tower erected itself in my head,
we couldn't find the lifts, climbed the stairs.

Of course there were fireworks.

We stared at each other, rare exhibits in the Louvre –
you licked my *Mona Lisa* smile right off.

Of course we were both in imaginary Chanel.

We drank warm cider and ate pancakes, yours flambéed.
I got drunk, my tights laddered on both legs.

Of course we experienced tachycardia at the Moulin Rouge.

Our hotel, a boxed macaron on a navy boulevard –
we spun around in the dark outside, rain-dizzy.

Of course we slept at the Ritz.

Our little room tucked into the corner, a pink
pocket you slipped into that night.

Of course our fingers hunted for change.

In the mirrored elevator I couldn't meet your eye, I
crushed you into the laminated sample menu and died.

Of course it was only *la petite mort.*

BURN BABY, BURN

Did you know
that in Dante's *Inferno*
those who are false
end up in the eighth circle?

I like to imagine you there

in that evil orbit
weighed down and whipped
while I sit mutely on the bus
and it's still dark outside.

Thursdays are dull

usually I'm more forgiving but
darling, as the wheels go round
and round I'd thrill to hear
your bones crunch underneath.

MOBY-DICK

I never imagined that
in Arrowhead when I encouraged you to purchase
a set of engravings of the whale and Ahab that
they would end up six years later
in your airy Dublin apartment,

the one that you share with your Canadian girlfriend.

'Look,' you say when I visit
for the first time,
'we hung the whale above the fireplace.'
You have left the bedroom door open and I see
the other picture hangs easily over your white bed.

Life, perverse origami, folds and twists and shapes itself
so that in your apartment, my coat lies on your crisp sheets.
I watch it from the living room,
beached upon that ivory shore,
as I sip weak tea.

ON THE PUBLICATION OF *LES TERRES DU CIEL* (1884)

Dearest Camille,

I want you; I want you to take skin
from my back, my shoulders,
skin that covers my breasts.

The highwayman James Allen
covered a memoir with his hide, a gift
to a brave man he tried to rob.

The judicial proceedings of murderer
John Horwood are sandwiched
in his largest organ.

Anatomy texts are bound
with skin of dissected cadavers,
de Sade's *Justine et Juliette* has nipples.

I want to cradle *Les Terres du Ciel*
between my thighs, my soul
passing from planet to planet. To be

a citizen of the sky, cross its universe faster
than light, touch that jagged lunar crescent,
see Saturn glowing scarlet and sapphire.

You think me frivolous, a society woman.
You are wrong. I know constellations will reign
in noise before existence, stars burn after our sun

dies. I want a world covered with telescopes.
Earth is only a chapter, less than that, a phrase,
less still, a word. Let me carry it.

SMELL DATING

They came in ten tiny transparent plastic bags,
the torn armpits of strangers' T-shirts still humming
with their owners' un-deodorised sweat. *Trust*

yourself the website said, *your nose knows*.
In the kitchen I take each sample out,
unfurl it like a napkin at a fancy restaurant,

hold each swatch to my nose, huff deeply.
This one smells of bubble gum, another of the sea,
still another of rotting wood. The white-T they sent

me hung from my body for three days, grew slack like old
skin. I tried to embrace my natural scent but was careful
where I went, didn't exercise. Leaving the samples

to pine on the table I go to the bedroom, pull back the covers,
press the pillow to my face. *Surrender yourself to the poignant
experience of body odour,* the website said. It smells like me.

IN HEPTONSTALL

I find you (it's not a competition) sprouting tulips, a jar of pens.
I lay three daffodils; my new husband kneels to take a photograph.
We debate the portent of honeymoon snaps of dead poets' graves.

In the picture the wind messes with my hair, light makes me squint.
On-screen I am already in the past. I apologise to your neighbour,
step on his plot to get closer. My husband wisely wanders off.

I talk aloud, resist the weird urge to lie on top of you,
as if we'd share something else but soil. I don't think we'd have gotten on.
I tell you about my wedding, the poems I write on train tickets, on receipts,

this poem. I do cry, relieved where you're buried is wild and fierce,
that there are red tulips licking your name in metal and stone, hungry.
My husband returns waving a tissue like a white flag.

HOW TO SKIN A DOGFISH

I've seen so many of you, all washed-up,
perished from cold and salt, mummified
on the beach. The world's too big
for you, or you're too small.

Walking these straight sands
my husband shows me how tricky
you are to skin, that it's worth it
for your sweet, flaky meat.

He mimes how he would slice round
your head, cut off your poisonous fins,
peel the skin back, standing
on your face for leverage.

The skin comes off smoothly, he says,
and spiny white dogfish is delicious fried.
Not a job for a wimp like me. Watching the tide
locked in its unbreakable pattern, I shiver

at the repetition: your dogfish bodies
on the beach, my scavenger brain coming out
in goosebumps, combing the sand – opportunistic
feeders, eating whatever we can sink our teeth into.

HUNGER STRIKES VICTORIA KENNEFICK

She punches her stomach loose, blind-
naked like a baby mole.
In the shower she cannot wash herself clean
the way she'd like. Rid herself
of useless molecules. Would that she
could strip her bones,
be something
neat,
complete.
Useful.

To eat or not to eat,
switch table sides.
Stuff cheese sandwiches
and chocolate blocks into a wide
moist orifice. Or, alternatively
zip that mouth
closed like a jacket,
a body already
contained within.
It doesn't need
to feed.

But I have set a table for us all.
For us all, a feast!
On a vast, smooth cloth, already soiled.
Let's take a seat, eat our fill.
You know you want to,
dig in.

FAMILY PLANNING

You are tugging at my skirt, aged two,
wanting a toy, a spoon from the drawer.

You are a few months old, just able
to hold your big old baby head up on that teensy neck.

It is your birthday. I am sweating and empty; you are
greasy-white with vernix, rising and falling with my breath.

I survived and you did too, your father is crying.
We are a little family, neat as a pin. Except

you are still waiting, Portia or Lucia or May
in parts. I carry a tiny piece I secrete

so secretly every month, you grow impatient when water
turns that warm and brilliant shade. It is alive

while you are not. Daughter-to-be, if you could form
your hands into little fists you would bang on my womb,

that carpet-lined waiting room, but your father has your fingers
and I have wrapped your nails up so you can't rip me to ribbons.

We keep you apart, even as we come together, but I hear
him whisper your name, soft as blame in his sleep.

INTERCESSION TO ST ANTHONY

I am on my knees.
Find him –

Was that his bald head bobbing,
a candle-flame on my horizon –
the scar a tell, upside-down horse shoe
with all the luck spilled out.

The earth is eating
my family up –
it practises sucking at the soles
of my shoes. I can't resist pressing

my fingers into its soil, smearing muck
on my face, war paint. But I'm a loser,
my father died when I wasn't looking.
Careless, I've mislaid

my keys again. I buzz around,
a stupid bluebottle bouncing off
walls, where are they?
Where is he? I hit my head on a shelf.

I swear I have left my body –
then you let me see, St Anthony,
I'm broke from you and now
a gift given back –

a missing leopard print sock,
the lost gold earring,
my keys and now –
his clear white bones

licked clean, burning the ground.
I get up; the scar
dissolved, the candle quenched,
there. There he is –

GUEST ROOM

I change the duvet cover like she showed me,
inside-out, corner-to-corner; lift it over
my head, seams must be flush.
I fold a pyramid of towels jewelled
with tiny soaps, body lotions borrowed
from hotels, the red hot-water-bottle
I'll fill later – her rubber husband.
I *Shake n' Vac* the carpet forest fresh; suck
spiders' webs from each corner, grey
and fuzzy, thick as pelts.

My mother's perfume sniffs out
that I did not iron the sheets.
Her nightdress pressed into a perfect square,
a village of potions on the bedside locker.
My heart sags, an empty hammock
yawning for the cradle of her arms,
the animal comfort of her wolf-fur
coat. I hear her pottering in my kitchen,
tidying. I turn out the light; night
cracks its knuckles.

Á LA CARTE

In the restaurant
I watch you slice a hunk of meat
on porcelain.

Your winking knife presses
to relieve muscle from fat,
soft as toothless gums.

The steak wants you to eat it,
is begging even, like a palm.
I have not eaten meat

all my adult life – its juice
an embarrassment, but now
I cannot look away. The fillet

pulsates on your plate.
Would you like a bite? you say,
extending a sliver on a fork

towards my lips. In front
of me, leaves, nuts, seeds.
To be honest, I say, *I'm starving.*

OPEN YOUR MOUTH

As a toddler,
        Krishna ate clay
                for fun,
                        his worried mother
                                prying open his mouth
                                        felt herself whirling in space, lost
                                                inside that baby mouth
                                        the whole universe,
                                moving and unmoving creation.
                        The earth, its mountains and oceans,
                moon and stars,
        planets and regions
and the child Krishna
        with his wide-open mouth
                and her kneeling
                        before him, and within
        that mouth another
universe
        and within
                that mouth
                        another

universe
        and within
                that mouth
                        another

universe
        and within
                that mouth
                        another.

Eat,

      he said, holding out
          the mud

              in his chubby hand,
                and so on,

                        or we both starve.
                    She opened wide, kept
                her tongue flat. The substance
          was thick

        and active.
She did not know

      what she was

        tasting,

           she swallowed

             and felt

                full.

PRAYER TO AUDREY HEPBURN

O Blessed Audrey of the feline eye-flick, jutting
bones, slim-hipped androgyny of war-time rationing, I've missed
your nightly visitations. I summoned you, carefully cutting
around your monochrome face in mother's fashion magazines,
pointing the scissors away from myself as I had been taught,
your name an incantation on my lips. I stuck those pieces
of you to my pink walls with rolled-up Sellotape, and waited.
You came, sheathed in black with the posture of a reed.
Hypnotised, I prayed to you for grace, that I could sew
my mouth closed like a doll, be a sculpture made of skin.

Years later and there's a person growing in my uterus,
my body a building-site. I intercede to you again, snip around
your slinky silhouette. In scissors' blades I see myself,
thirteen, when you fall out of the shadows. Oh Audrey!
Can't stay, you hiss. You stare at me with saucer eyes. *I am hungry*, you say.
Hungry, like you. I can't help but laugh – I am too big to be a woman.
You lean over the bed; I am conscious of my pudgy belly,
my rat's nest hair, but you take my face in your hands, kiss me hard,
pushing your gorgeous tongue across the length of mine.
Afterwards, our seams popping, we shriek with laughter.

ACKNOWLEDGEMENTS

With thanks to the following publications where a number of these poems, or earlier versions of them, have been published: *Poetry Magazine*, *The Poetry Review*, *Ambit*, *Poetry News*, *Poetry Ireland Review*, *The Stinging Fly*, *Prelude*, *Copper Nickel*, *The Manchester Review*, *Banshee*, *The High Window*, *Southword*, *The Irish Times* and *The Irish Examiner*. *Poems of Paris*, Everyman's Library Pocket Poets Series, 2019. Some poems also appeared in a pamphlet, *White Whale* (Southword Editions, 2015), winner of the Munster Literature Centre Fool for Poetry Chapbook Competition and the Saboteur Award for Best Poetry Pamphlet.

The completion of this manuscript was generously supported by a Next Generation Artist Bursary from the Arts Council of Ireland, a Sarah Lawrence College Summer Seminar for Writers Scholarship, a Words Ireland Mentorship, a Winter Tangerine Online Fellowship, a Kerry County Council Bursary to spend time at the Tyrone Guthrie Centre and a Listowel Writers' Week New Writers' Residential Award at Cill Rialaig. Thank you all.

My sincere and deepest gratitude to Colette Bryce, Rebecca Goss and especially the tireless and endlessly inspiring, John McAuliffe. Brilliant poets but also generous, insightful and empathetic mentors. I am so fortunate to have had the benefit of their time, expertise and kindness.

I am grateful for the support of Principal Kerry Harkin, Deputy Principal Seán Costelloe and all my friends and students in Presentation Secondary School Milltown.

For all the books, midnight readings and endless belief and patience, thank you to the Fitzgerald and Kennefick families in this world and the next: my beloved parents, Robert and Úna, my brilliant sisters, Louise (my first editor), Fiona, Suzi and their families. My brother Stephen and his family. To Donal (Dods), Peadar, Nora, Cáit, Bernie, Colm, Joe, Gerald and to all my Margarets on both sides, to the Murphy clan, my love and appreciation always. I am so lucky. For time, space and encouragement thank you to Jo and Harry, and Kate.

Thank you to Noel O'Regan for reading, and re-reading, and re-reading with such sensitivity and care. I owe you several! Here's to Braintrust! To the English Literature Society UCC and AFKAM back in the day – cheers, love and poetry forever. A big shout out to the Munster Literature Centre for the many opportunities extended to me and their continued support. My sincere gratitude and love to all at Listowel Writers' Week, thank you for making this blow-in feel like she belongs. Long may you reign!

To my gorgeous husband David, 'whatever is done / By only me is your doing, my darling'. And sweet Vivienne, you were right, as always. I love you both so much.